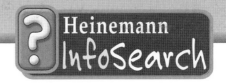

Stars and Constellations

Dr. Raman K. Prinja

Heinemann Library
Chicago, Illinois

© 2003 Reed Educational & Professional Publishing
Published by Heinemann Library,
an imprint of Reed Educational & Professional Publishing,
Chicago, Illinois

Customer Service 888-454-2279

Visit our website at www.heinemannlibrary.com

Designed by Jo Hinton-Malivoire
Originated by Dot Gradations Ltd.
Printed in Hong Kong, China by Wing King Tong

07 06 05 04 03
10 9 8 7 6 5 4 3 2 1

Library of Congress Cataloging-in-Publication
Prinja, Raman, 1961-
  Stars and constellations / Raman Prinja.
     v. cm. -- (The universe)
Includes bibliographical references and index.
Contents: Can I see all the stars in the sky? -- What are
constellations? -- What is a star made of? -- How far away are the
stars? -- How are stars made? -- How long do stars shine? -- How will
the stars end their lives? -- How do we study stars?
  ISBN 1-58810-916-X (hardcover) -- ISBN 1-40340-617-0 (pbk.)
  1. Stars--Juvenile literature. 2. Constellations--Juvenile
literature. [1. Stars.] I. Title. II. Series.
  QB801.7 .P75 2002
  523.8--dc21
                              2002004059

Acknowledgments
The author and publishers are grateful to the following for permission to reproduce copyright material:
pp. 4, 5, 6, 7, 11 (top), 14, 16, 17, 19, 20, 23, 24, 25, 26, 28/Science Photo Library; p. 11 (bottom)/Corbis;
p. 13/Bridgeman Art Library (National Library of Australia); pp. 18, 21, 27, 29/Science Photo Library/NASA.

Cover photograph reproduced with permission of Science Photo Library.

The author would like to thank Kamini, Vikas, Sachin and all his family for their support.

The publisher would like to thank Geza Gyuk and Diana Challis of the Adler Planetarium for their comments in the preparation of this book.

Some words are shown in **bold,** like this. You can find out what they mean by looking in the glossary.

Contents

Can I See All the Stars in the Sky?

On a moonless night, far away from the bright lights of houses and city streets, you can see about 3,000 sparkling stars. The tiny specks of light we see at night are from stars that are billions of miles away. Each of these stars has its own special life story. Our Sun is an ordinary star just like many others in the sky. It looks much bigger and brighter because it is a lot closer to us than the other stars. There are many distant stars in space that are much larger and more powerful than the Sun.

Thousands of stars can be seen on a dark, moonless night. The misty white band from top to bottom in this picture is called the Milky Way.

The stars that we see in our skies are only some of the hundreds of billions of stars that make up our **galaxy.** The rest are too faint or far away to be seen with just our eyes. A galaxy is a huge collection of stars held together by the force of **gravity.** There are perhaps 100 billion galaxies in the **universe.**

The galaxy that is home to our **solar system** and to all the stars we see in the sky, is called the Milky Way. It gets its name from a misty white band of millions of stars that stretches across the sky.

This is a picture of the Whirlpool Galaxy, which looks a little like our Milky Way Galaxy. Galaxies are made of billions of stars.

The milky band that makes up the Milky Way can really only be seen in dark skies far away from city lights. The stars in our galaxy give us some of the most amazing sights in space.

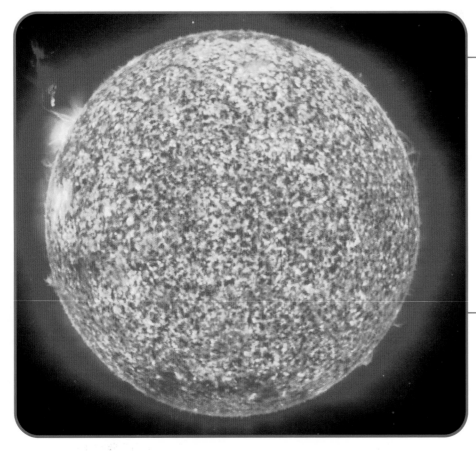

*All stars, like the Sun, are huge balls mostly made of boiling hot **hydrogen** gas. The stars have no solid surface. They are very different from rocky planets like Earth.*

What are "wandering stars?"

Thousands of years ago, people noticed that five "stars" in the sky moved much faster than all the others. The ancient Greeks worshipped them as five gods. Today we know that these "wandering stars" are not stars at all.They are the planets Mercury, Venus, Mars, Jupiter, and Saturn.

Stars don't really move during the night

If you go out after dark and choose a bright star, then come back and look for it a few hours later, you will find that it is no longer where you first saw it! It will now be toward your west. Just as the Sun and Moon rise in the east and set in the west, so do the stars.

The stars aren't really traveling east to west every night. They only seem to move because the Earth, on which you are standing, is spinning on its **axis.**

As the Earth spins on its axis, the stars seem to move around us. To create this image of the stars moving across the sky, the camera was left on over a period of time.

What Are Constellations?

Thousands of years ago, our ancestors began to recognize patterns, or groups, of stars in the sky at night. Year after year, they could see the patterns rising and setting. These patterns of stars are called **constellations.**

Constellations are not real. They are imaginary ways of grouping stars that poets, farmers, and **astronomers** have made up over the past 6,000 years.

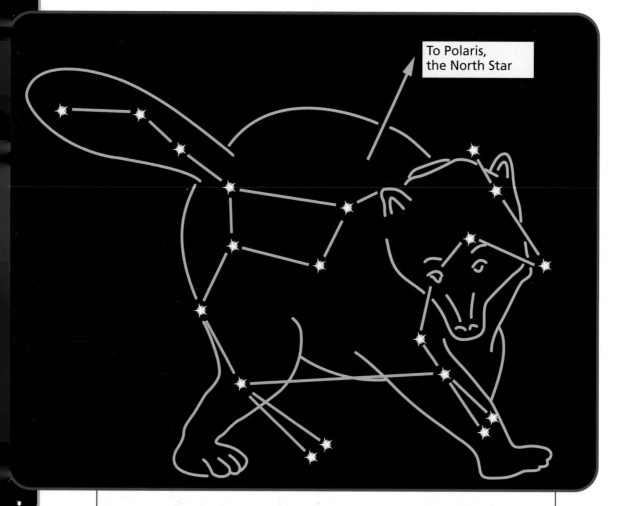

To Polaris, the North Star

This diagram shows the constellation of Ursa Major, or the Great Bear, which can be seen all year. The best view is in the spring.

Connecting the dots

Ancient people formed the shapes of animals or creatures out of the star patterns. They imagined lines drawn between a few stars to make shapes from stories in their **myths.** They were playing connect-the-dots with the stars. For example, the constellation of Draco is named after the picture of a dragon that appears after connecting lines between at least fifteen different stars.

Finding constellations

The constellations were first made up a long time ago. Today, in cities with bright street lights, it can be hard to make them out. Also, most of the constellations don't really look much like the people or animals after which they were named. So don't worry if you can't find the bull in Taurus or the lion in Leo.

Earth's **equator** is an imaginary line that divides the planet into two halves, the northern **hemisphere** and the southern hemisphere. You will see a different set of constellations depending on if you live north or south of the equator.

Eighty-eight constellations

Today our entire sky is divided into 88 constellations. They join up to cover the whole sky, just as countries fill the map of a **continent** on Earth. Different cultures around the world have different amounts and names of constellations. Thousands of years ago, Chinese astronomers divided the sky into just 28 constellations.

Stars in the northern hemisphere

Here are four **constellations** you can look for if you live in the northern **hemisphere.**

In spring: Try to find the constellation called Ursa Major, or the Great Bear (shown on page 8). During spring it is high above the northeast **horizon.** Inside the pattern of the Great Bear is a smaller one made of seven stars called the Big Dipper.

This diagram shows the constellation of Cygnus, the swan.

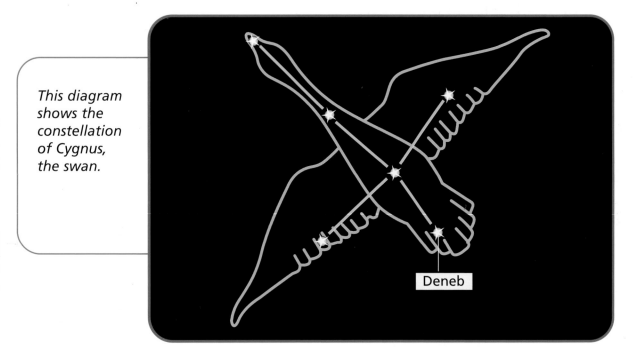

Deneb

In summer: During summer you can look for the constellation called Cygnus, which is the **Latin** name for swan. It rises high in the sky during the evenings. The brightest star in Cygnus is called Deneb, and it marks the tail of the swan.

In fall: An easy constellation to spot in fall is Cassiopeia. In Greek **myths,** a queen called Cassiopeia was placed among the stars by the seagod, Poseidon. Cassiopeia looks like a wide letter W, made of five bright stars. It is best seen high in northeastern skies during November. *In winter*: A beautiful constellation seen in winter is

This is the constellation of Orion, the hunter.

Orion. It is named after a great hunter in ancient Greek myths. Orion has the shape of a large rectangle, but it is meant to show the shape of the hunter! Three bright stars in a row make up the hunter's belt that holds a sword. Two bright red stars called Betelgeuse and Rigel mark the left shoulder and the right foot of the hunter.

Stars in the southern hemisphere

People living in the southern hemisphere can see 32 constellations in the skies. Many of these were named only a few hundred years ago when scientists and explorers went from the north to south of the **equator** for the first time.

The most famous of these constellations is called Crux, or the Southern Cross. It even appears on the national flags of Australia and New Zealand.

The national flag of Australia shows the constellation of the Southern Cross.

How Do People Use Constellations?

Constellations can be very useful for finding stars. On a dark, cloudless night you can see about 3,000 stars with your eyes (and millions more with a telescope). Trying to tell which star is which can be very difficult. The constellations help us pick out the bright stars by breaking up the sky into parts. This is similar to finding towns and cities on a map when a country is divided into regions or states.

Birds use the stars, too

Some birds can **migrate** thousands of miles from one part of the globe to another. How do the birds find their way? While some use features like rivers, coasts, and mountains, other birds watch the stars to find their way. On clear nights, birds such as the indigo bunting can travel by watching patterns of stars in the sky. Sailors also used the constellations to find their way.

This beautiful indigo bunting bird was photographed in Texas.

For hundreds of years, **astronomers** used the positions of the stars and constellations to find out the exact time. They used special telescopes that could not be moved from side to side. Every time Earth completes one turn on its **axis,** the same stars

Sailors used to watch the stars to work out where they were and what direction they needed to sail.

appear in front of the telescope. Astronomers can read the stars to tell the time, just as we would read the numbers on a clock.

How did ancient people use constellations?

Ancient people used the constellations to tell the time of year. They noticed where groups of stars were at different times of the year. Since different constellations can be seen during the year, they can be used to tell what month it is. This was a big help to farmers. Using the constellations, they knew it was time to plant the crops or harvest them.

What Is a Star Made Of?

People have always wondered what the stars are and how they were made. It is only in the past 100 years or so that scientists have begun to understand what the stars are made of, how they work, and how they change.

What makes the stars shine?

Stars are giant balls of incredibly hot gas. They are mostly made of **hydrogen** gas and don't have any solid surfaces. Stars have different regions, or layers. The outer layers are the only ones we can see directly, and they have temperatures of about 5,400 to 54,000 °F (3,000 to 30,000 °C).

The hydrogen gas in the center, or core, of a star is even hotter. It is being squeezed, and as this happens, it gets hotter. Some cores are more than 27 million °F (15 million °C). The energy that is made in this boiling hot core is what makes the stars and our Sun shine.

This picture shows the supergiant star called Betelgeuse, which is part of the constellation of Orion.

Hot stars, cool stars

There are two things that you can easily notice about stars in the night sky. First, they are not all the same color. Some stars are blueish, some are yellow-white, and others are reddish. The stars have different colors because they have different temperatures. The Sun is a medium-hot, yellow-white star. The blueish stars are much hotter than the Sun, and the red stars are cooler. Blue stars are usually younger than the red stars.

The second thing to notice is that some stars are brighter than others. Stars can appear brighter in the sky because they are more powerful. The may also appear brighter because they are much nearer to us (like the Sun). In just the same way, the light from a flashlight can seem bright either because the battery inside is strong, or because the flashlight is held near to you.

How big are the stars?

Our **galaxy** has hundreds of billions stars of many different sizes. Although the Sun is almost 865,000 miles (1.4 million kilometers) wide, it is just a medium sized star. There are giant stars in space that are 100 times larger than the Sun. There are also dwarf stars that are 100 times smaller.

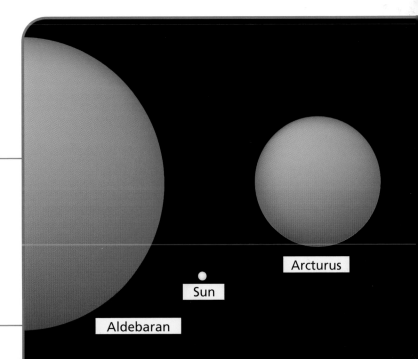

This diagram shows the size of the Sun in comparison with Arcturus, a **red giant** star, and Aldebaran, a **supergiant** star.

Arcturus

Sun

Aldebaran

How Far Away Are the Stars?

The Sun is 93 million miles (150 million kilometers) away from us. Most of the other stars are millions of times farther away. Light travels faster that anything we know. It moves at 186,000 miles (300,000 kilometers) per second, but still takes 8 minutes to reach us from the Sun.

Light takes around four years to reach us from the next nearest star. Remember, there are at least 100 billion other stars in the Milky Way. It would take almost 100,000 years for light to reach us from the farthest stars in the Milky Way. The light shining from billions of stars in a **galaxy** next to ours, called the Andromeda Galaxy, takes 2 million years to reach us.

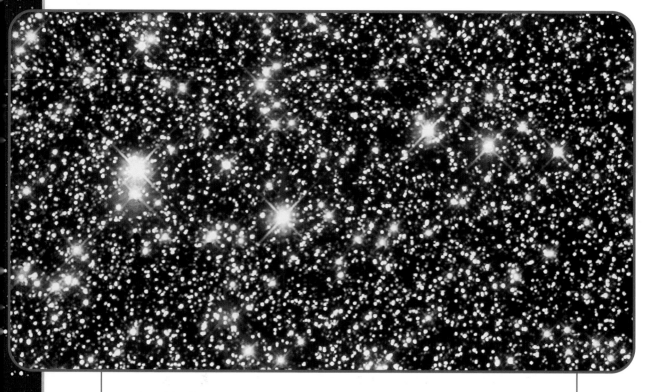

This dazzling mixture of different stars was seen using the Hubble Space Telescope. The stars have different colors, depending on their temperatures. Most blue stars are young and hot, while red stars are older and cooler.

The Milky Way and Andromeda are just two of the billions and billions of galaxies that make up the **universe.** It would take more than 10 billion years for light to reach us from stars in the most distant galaxies that we can see.

*This spiral galaxy is very similar in size and shape to our own galaxy, the Milky Way, but is 15 million **light years** away from Earth.*

A scale model

Imagine Earth scaled down to the size of the period at the end of this sentence. On this scale, the Sun would be about the size of a golf ball, placed about 10 feet (3 meters) away. The next nearest star would be 540 miles (870 kilometers) away in our model. The entire Milky Way would be a giant plate that is 12 million miles (20 million kilometers) wide. Remember, this is on a scale where Earth is just the size of a dot on this page. Just think, there are billions of other galaxies much farther away in the universe.

How Are Stars Made?

Stars are born somewhere in our **galaxy** every year. Stars are made out of huge clouds of **hydrogen** gas and dust. These giant clouds are called **nebulae.** *Nebulae* is the **Latin** name for mist.

The nebulae can be a million times bigger than the distance between the Sun and the farthest planet in our **solar system,** Pluto. This distance is almost 3,670 million miles (5,900 million kilometers). Each nebula can hold enough gas and dust to make thousands of stars. The **constellation** of Orion has a star-making nebula in it.

Squashed by gravity

The gas in a nebula is slowly squashed together by the force of **gravity,** a little like the way you might gather loose snow to make a hard snowball. After a few million years, a lot of gas in space is brought together into a tightly squashed ball. This giant ball becomes hotter and hotter.

New stars are being made in these huge pillars of gas and dust called the Eagle Nebula.

When a star is born

Slowly, the temperature at the center of the ball of gas reaches millions of degrees. Then something special happens to this very hot and tightly packed gas. The hydrogen is changed into a different gas called helium. This is called a **nuclear fusion reaction.**

Whenever nuclear fusion happens in the ball of hot gas, a lot of energy is released. This is the energy that makes a star shine brilliantly. When the nuclear reactions start, a star is born.

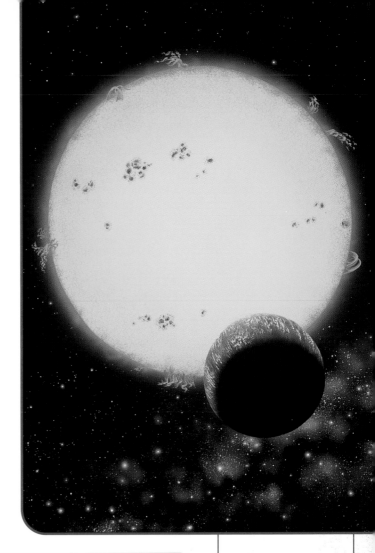

An artist's idea of a Jupiter-like planet orbiting another star, like our Sun.

Where do planets come from?

Some gas and dust are usually left over after a star has been made. Over millions of years, this extra material is gathered into small clumps by the force of gravity. The clumps then crash into each other and grow larger. Finally, these clumps of rocky material become planets that **orbit** the newly born star. Scientists think there may be many millions of stars with their own planets in our galaxy.

How Long Do Stars Shine?

The stars in the sky are not all the same. Some of them are young, many are middle-aged, and a few are very old. Stars don't live forever. After they are born, they change over billions of years and then they die. A bright star that you can see in a **constellation** today might not be there billions of years from now.

Life stories

When a star is first made in a **nebula,** it can be a massive heavyweight star or a small lightweight one. The life stories of these two types of stars are different.

Lightweight stars like the Sun

The Sun is a lightweight star, born about 4.5 billion years ago. It shines constantly by using fuel in the form of **hydrogen** gas in **nuclear fusion reactions.** About 5 billion years from now this fuel supply will run out.

This group of stars is in the constellation Gemini.

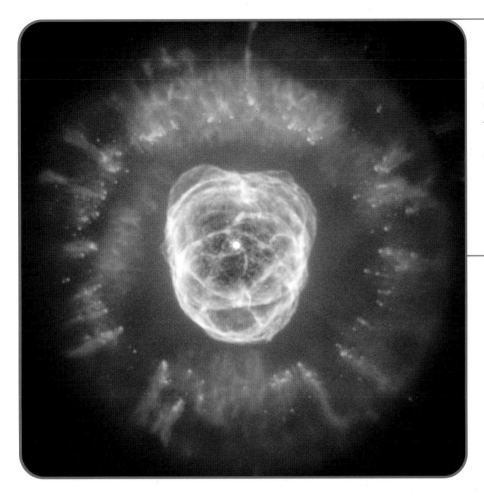

This is a planetary nebula called the Eskimo. The dying star began throwing out material about 10,000 years ago.

When any star runs out of fuel, big changes take place. In around 5 billion years, the Sun will swell up and become a huge, but cooler, star. Because its temperature will be lower, it will have a reddish color. These types of stars are called **red giants.** When the Sun is a red giant it will swallow the planet Mercury and perhaps even Venus. Earth's **atmosphere** will be scorched and the oceans will boil away. All life on Earth will come to an end.

After they become red giants, light stars puff away a lot of their gas. The layers blown away by the star make an object called a **planetary nebula.** It is made of hot gas that was once part of the outer regions of the star. There are many beautiful and colorful planetary nebulae in our galaxy today. A planetary nebula is a sign that a star is dying.

All that is left behind of the star is its small core, or central part. The core has been crushed by **gravity.** It is now a tiny star about the size of Earth called a **white dwarf.** It is made of very tightly packed carbon material. More than 5 billion years from now, the Sun will end its life as a white dwarf. The white dwarf star starts out at nearly 180,000 °F (100,000 °C). It cools, over billions of years, to become just a cold and dark object in space.

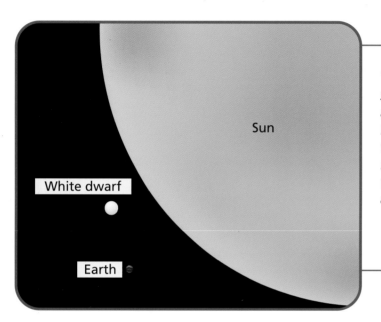

White dwarf

Sun

Earth

This diagram shows the size of a white dwarf star in comparison with the Sun and the Earth. The life of the Sun will end as a white dwarf star.

Stars much heavier than the Sun

There are massive stars in space that are between 10 to 100 times heavier than the Sun. The lives of these stars are much shorter than that of the Sun. This is because they are very powerful stars, and they burn their supply of **hydrogen** fuel very quickly.

When it is only about 10 million years old, a massive star can already be heading toward an explosive death. Its outer layers swell up. The star becomes a **supergiant** that may be hundreds of times larger than the Sun is today. Two stars called Betelgeuse and Rigel in the **constellation** of Orion are supergiant stars.

Out with a bang

The supergiant star will end its life with a huge explosion called a **supernova.** When the star's supply of fuel for **nuclear fusion reactions** has run out, the supernova will blast the star apart in just a few seconds. This is one of the most powerful explosions known in the **universe.** The huge star is almost totally destroyed.

The only thing left behind after this amazing supernova is the squeezed core, crushed by the force of gravity. The once huge star may end up as either a **neutron star** or a **black hole.** We take a look at both of these incredible objects in the next chapter.

Huge stars will shatter in violent supernova explosions like the one shown in this computer drawing.

How Will the Stars End Their Lives?

Lightweight stars like the Sun end their lives as **white dwarf** stars. Much heavier stars end their lives as **neutron stars** or **black holes**. These are three of the strangest and most mysterious objects in space.

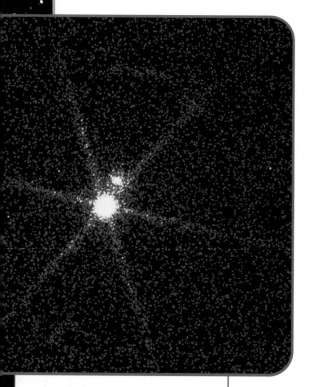

The brightest star in the night sky is called Sirius. The tiny star above it is a white dwarf star.

Earth-sized white dwarf

A white dwarf star is usually only slightly larger than Earth, yet it weighs nearly half as much as the Sun. This means that the gas in the star is squeezed very tightly together. If you could bring a spoonful of white dwarf material to Earth, it would weigh as much as a tractor!

More than half of the stars in our **galaxy** will end up as white dwarf stars. Because they are so small and faint, **astronomers** have to use powerful telescopes to find them.

Neutron stars

A neutron star is formed after a star that weighs up to 20 times more than the Sun explodes as a **supernova**. A neutron star is even stranger than a white dwarf. All the **matter** in this tiny star has been squeezed by **gravity** into a ball the size of a city, perhaps only six miles (ten kilometers) across. A spoonful of its material would weigh as much as a large mountain on Earth.

Black holes—no way out!

A black hole forms after a star that weighs more than 20 times the weight of the Sun, blows up in a supernova explosion. Black holes are the most mysterious objects in space. Gravity squeezes the leftovers of the dying star into an incredibly tiny space. If you could take the Earth and crush it into the size of a grape, you would end up with a black hole!

A black hole is a region of space in which the pull of gravity is so strong that nothing can ever escape from it. Even light, which is the fastest thing in the universe, cannot get out. So they don't shine at all and that's why they are called black holes.

An artist's idea of swirling hot gas and dust being sucked into a black hole.

How Do We Study Stars?

Scientists who study the stars are called **astronomers.** To learn more about what the stars are made of and how they change, astronomers use giant telescopes. The telescopes let them see very faint objects in great detail.

The bigger and higher, the better

The largest telescopes in the world are almost 33 feet (10 meters) across. They are usually placed on very high mountains, far away from bright city lights.

Even at these great heights, the Earth's **atmosphere** can ruin the view of the stars. The air is always shaking and moving and this is what makes the stars twinkle at night. This movement makes the stars look blurry through telescopes on the ground.

It is much better if the telescope is placed above Earth's atmosphere in space. This is exactly what was done for one special telescope.

These giant telescopes, called Keck I and II, have been built on a mountain 14,000 feet (4200 meters) high in Hawaii.

The Hubble Space Telescope

On April 24, 1990, the Hubble Space Telescope was launched into space on a **Space Shuttle** rocket. The telescope is in **orbit** 370 miles (600 kilometers) above Earth. It is controlled using radio signals sent from Earth. Since 1990, astronauts have visited the telescope to add new parts and make repairs.

The Hubble Space Telescope is very powerful and allows scientists to clearly see objects that are far away in space. Many of the pictures in this book were taken using this telescope.

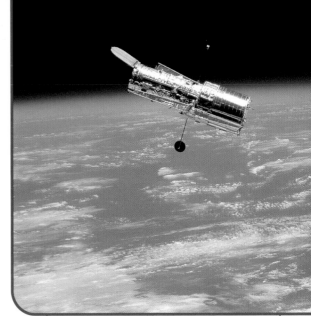

A view of the Hubble Space Telescope floating in orbit around the Earth.

The first telescopes

- Galileo Galilei was the first person to use a telescope for **astronomy.** In 1611, he used it to discover that the Sun had **dark spots.**
- In 1672, Sir Isaac Newton made the first telescope that used mirrors instead of lenses. This idea was very important.
- Scientists then learned that the width of the mirror in a telescope was more important than the telescope's length.
- In 1673, Johannes Hevelius built a telescope that was 140 feet (42.5 meters) long. It was hard to use because even the slightest wind would make it flutter.
- By 1948, a 16-foot (5-meter) wide telescope was built on Palomar Mountain in California.
- Today, some of the best telescopes in the world are on the island of Mauna Kea in Hawaii and on mountain ranges in Chile in South America.

Fact File

Here are some interesting facts about stars:

Galaxy of stars—Our Milky Way galaxy is made of hundreds of billions of stars. There are many different types of stars in our Galaxy.

Nearest—The nearest star to Earth after the Sun is called Proxima Centauri. It is still 270,000 times farther away from us than the Sun. If you imagine traveling in a spaceship at a speed of 30,000 miles (50,000 kilometers) per hour, it would take almost 90,000 years to reach Proxima Centauri!

Brightest—The brightest star in the sky after the Sun is called Sirius. It is in the **constellation** of Canis Major.

Most powerful—One of the most powerful stars known is called the Pistol star. It shines with 10 million times more power than the Sun.

This is a doomed star called Eta Carina. One day it will explode as a ***supernova.***

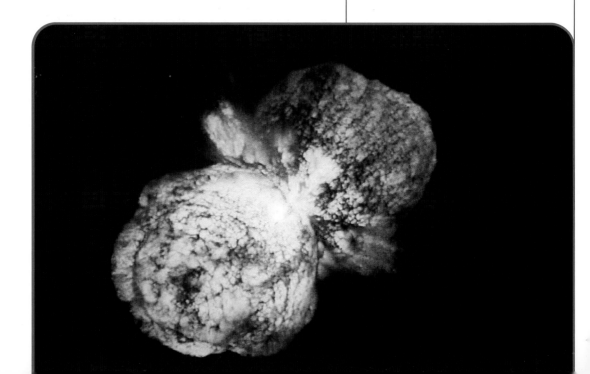

The universe has billions and billions galaxies, and each galaxy has billions of stars.

Largest—The largest known star is a **supergiant** star called Mu Cephei. It is around 3,700 times bigger than the Sun. If Mu Cephei were placed at the center of our **solar system,** it would probably swallow all the planets as far out as Saturn, and almost reach the planet Uranus.

Hottest—The hottest known star is a **white dwarf** star at the center of a **planetary nebula** called NGC2440. This tiny star's outer layers have a temperature of 360,000 ° Fahrenheit (200,000 °Celsius), which is 30 times hotter than the Sun.

Glossary

astronomers scientists who study objects in space, such as planets and stars

astronomy scientific study of space, including planets, stars and galaxies

atmosphere layers of gases that surround a planet

axis imaginary line around which a planet or moon spins

black hole invisible object in space that forms when a very massive star is crushed by gravity

carbon element in all living things

constellation imaginary pattern or picture formed in the sky by a group of stars

dark spots cooler patches sometimes seen on the Sun, also known as sunspots

equator imaginary line around the middle of Earth

galaxy collection of millions or billions of stars, gas, and dust

gravity force that pulls all objects towards the surface of Earth, or any other planet, moon, or star

hemisphere half of the Earth between the North or South Pole and the equator

Latin language of the ancient Romans

light year distance that light travels in one year (nearly 6 trillion miles)

matter substance that all things are made of

myth old, made-up story

nebulae clouds of gas and dust in space

nuclear fusion reaction process where light substances are joined to make heavier ones, releasing enormous amounts of energy

neutron star squashed remains of a dead star, which spins very quickly

orbit path taken by an object as it moves around another body (planet or star)

planetary nebula cloud of gas that surrounds stars like the Sun when they run out of energy and begin to die

red giant cool star that has swollen to a much larger size than the Sun is today

solar system the group of nine planets and other objects orbiting the Sun forms our solar system

Space Shuttle vehicle used by people to travel into space and orbit Earth

supergiant very swollen star that may be thousands of times larger than the Sun

supernova very bright and violent explosion of a huge star

universe all of space and its contents of matter and energy, including all planets, galaxies, and stars

white dwarf very hot, small object formed when stars run out of energy and die

More Books to Read

Crosswell, Ken. *Sees the Stars: Your First Guide to the Night Sky.* Honesdale, Penn.: Boyd Mills Press, 2000.

Prinja, Dr. Raman K. *The Sun.* Chicago: Heinemann, 2003.

Vogt, Gregory. *Stars and Constellations.* Austin, Tex.: Raintree Steck-Vaughn, 2001.

Index